Budgeting:

How to Make a Budget and Manage Your Money and Personal Finances like a Pro

Jenny Holmquist

Contents

Introduction

I want to thank you and commend you for opening the book, *"Budgeting: How to Make a Budget and Manage Your Money and Personal Finances like a Pro"*.

This book contains actionable steps and strategies on how to budget and manage your finances like a pro.

Many people are neck deep in debt and have very bad credit reports today because of lack of proper financial planning.

You see; the difference between the rich and the poor is that the rich have been able to quickly learn and understand that money management is a skill that must be carefully mastered. No matter how rich you are or how much money you make, you cannot stay wealthy for a long time if you don't know how to manage your money.

Earning a lot of money is not what makes you rich; knowing how to manage and utilize your money well is what would make you a wealthy person. As such, the art of budgeting is one of the most important things that you must master if you want to achieve financial freedom.

In this book, we break down the art of budgeting and personal finance in a way that is very easy to understand. When you are done reading this book, you will be able to create, monitor, and adjust your personal budget like a pro.

Thanks again for opening this book, I hope you enjoy it!

Chapter 1: Budgeting Basics
What Is A Budget?

Many people wrongly think of budgeting as something that is only meant for broke people; something that you do when you are low on cash or when you have many expenses that exceed the money you have at your disposal.

But this is a wrong idea; budgeting is not only for broke people or for when you don't have access to enough money. It is something that everyone should do whether he or she is rich or poor.

Imagine living in a country without a budget? Or working with a company that has no clear financial plan? Of course, that would be a very disorganized and backward country or company.

Everybody needs a financial budget whether individual, company, or country as it is an invaluable tool that can be used to manage money and other resources. Budgeting helps you to pay close attention to your income and expenditure and most importantly, budgeting can make you rich.

Before I go on to teach you some of the other major reasons why you must have a budget, let me define what a budget is in simple terms. A budget is an itemized list or summary of all your projected income and expenses for a specific period of time. It details your income and how you plan to spend it. With a budget, you can get a concrete and vivid breakdown of the money you are making and how you are spending it.

Why You Must Have A Budget

There are many reasons why it is important for everyone to have a budget but the most important ones include:

1. **Helps you identify wasteful expenditure**: Have you ever had that feeling that you don't know where your money goes? That's most likely because of a lot of wasteful expenditure on your part because you do not plan your expenditure properly and you end up spending your money spontaneously. Budgeting can help you become much more financially responsible and avoid wasteful spending and impulse buying.

2. **Helps you adapt to financial changes**: It's true that the only constant thing in life is change. A single person might decide to get married, a married couple might decide to have children and a person who has no car might decide to purchase one. All of these are changes that would have an impact on your finances. However, with a clear budget, you can avoid panicking when such changes occur because you would be able to incorporate those changes into your budget easily.

3. **To achieve financial growth**: To achieve financial growth, you need to save and invest. Without adequate financial planning and budgeting, you might be unable to save money and probably never invest. However, when you have a budget, you are able to adjust your expenses to

accommodate some savings, which you can then invest to achieve financial growth.

4. **Reduces Stress**: Nothing stresses a person as much as emergency financial expenses that they are unable to meet up with. Nobody wishes for emergencies but they happen anyway, which is why it is important to always be prepared for such expenses. With a good budget, you are able to leave out some money to take care of such emergences if they arise.

5. **Helps you plan for short and long-term goals**: Budgeting will also make it easier for you to plan for and set aside some money to take care of your long-term goals as well as your short-term goals.

6. **Helps you use your money well**: When you are creating your budget, you are thinking clearly and mapping out your expenditures to match your goals. You are different from a spontaneous spender who just spends money according to their emotional and sentimental needs. Therefore, with a clear budget, you are able to plan and use your money very well.

7. **Prevents Debts**: Having a personal budget also helps you to learn to live within your means so that you can avoid debts that may ruin your financial standing in the future.

Now that you understand the benefits of a good budget, what then makes a good budget?

Elements Of A Personal Budget

Every good personal budget must have the following elements:

- **Income**: This details your earnings and the source of your earnings such as your wages and salaries, interests from investments, commissions and other sources of income. Income may be fixed (for those who earn salaries) or variable (for business people or people who do not earn specific income monthly).

- **Fixed Expenses**: These are expenditures that have a fixed sum such as rents, mortgage, loan repayments, and other similar expenses that can be easily predetermined.

- **Flexible/Variable Expenses**: Such expenses do not have fixed sums. They include expenses like phone bills, water bills, groceries, gasoline and so on.

- **Unplanned Expenses**: Every good budget must also have a section for unplanned or emergency expenses because if you don't plan for these expenditures, they will ruin your budget.

- **Savings and Investments**: Lastly, your budget should leave aside something for savings and investment so that you are able to grow your finances.

In the following chapter, we are going to look at creating a budget.

Chapter 2: How To Create A Personalized Financial Budget

Creating your own personal financial budget is very easy. In this chapter, you will find a detailed step by step procedure to follow in order to create a very good budget that suits your lifestyle and your personal needs.

Tools You Need

You don't need many tools to create a good budget. However, you do need the following:

- **A pen and paper**: It's always good to first plan your budget on pen and paper before transferring to any electronic media so that you can easily make corrections and adjustments by hand.

- **A Computer Spreadsheet**: The most recommended one is Microsoft Excel Spreadsheet. Microsoft Excel Spreadsheet can be used to make calculations without errors and helps you store your budget in electronic form.

- **Financial Planning Software**: You might not necessarily need this but it's a good tool to have. Financial planning software like Microsoft Money and Quicken have so many great features that would help to make your budgeting experience an interesting one. You can also find many other free software online.

How To Create A Budget

1. **Outline Your Goals**: First, you must have a clear idea of what your financial goals are. Are you trying to reduce your debts? Plan for your future or increase your wealth? When you have clear goals, it makes your budgeting easy. Financial goals can be categorized under three main headings; short-term goals, midterm goals and long-term goals.

   - **Short Term Financial Goals**: These include things that you wish to achieve within the year. A short-term goal is a goal that covers less than 1 year.

   - **Mid-Term Financial Goals**: These goals cover one to three years. What do you see yourself achieving in the next three years? Want to start your own business? Buy a house? Change your car? All these are mid-term financial goals.

   - **Long Term Financial Goals**: These goals cover a period of five years or more. For instance, if you want to retire in the next seven years, that is a long-term financial goal.

     Good financial goals must be SMART. This means that they must be:

     Specific: You must have a clear idea of what you want to achieve.

Measurable: You must know what it would cost.

Achievable: You must be able to achieve that goal within the period specified.

Relevant: It must be relevant to the overall plan for your life.

Time-Framed: Lastly, you must set a specific period of time during which you want to achieve these goals.

2. **Figure Out Your Income**: Where will the money you intend to spend come from? You must list all your sources of income and how much you are likely to earn monthly. If you are creating a joint budget for your family, you may need to add your spouses' income as well. Common sources of income include wages and salaries, interests and pensions. It is very important to ensure that the income you include in your budget is your after-tax income. Taxes are not for you to spend; they belong to the government so you cannot add them to your budget hence you must deduct taxes from your income before adding them to your budget.

3. **Figure out Your Expenses**: This is like the most important part of your budget as any errors here may ruin your budget. You may have to spend some time observing your personal spending pattern before you are able to create a realistic expense budget. However, some common expenses to include in your budget include:

- **Fixed Expenses**: Rent and any other expenditure that remains constant

- **Flexible Expenses**: Food, entertainment and other expenses that change monthly

- **Wants**: Things like eating out, movies, dates, and electronics.

- **Unplanned Expenses**: Expenses for emergencies or other unplanned items

- **Savings and Investment allowances**

- **Charitable donations**

4. **Find out the difference:** Once you figure out your income and expenses, all that is left is for you to add both figures and subtract your expenses from income. You can have either a budget surplus or deficit after your deductions.

   - **Budget Surplus:** You have a budget surplus if you get a positive number after deducting your expenses from the income. A budget surplus is a good sign and it means that you are living within your means. You can either save the surplus or invest it.

   - **Budget Deficit:** When you deduct your expenses from your income and arrive at a negative figure, it shows you have a budget deficit. This is a bad sign. It shows that your income can barely cover your expenses. If you notice that you have a budget deficit, you should work towards reducing your expenses or increasing your income.

In determining how much money to spend on different expenditure items, you can use the 50/20/30 rule. This rule entails spending 50% of your earnings on fixed costs. These are costs that don't vary from month to month such as rent, utilities, mortgage payment and such. 20% of your income should be allocated to financial obligations like saving for retirement or emergency fund then 30% should be used for flexible spending like entertainment, gas, groceries, and such. Use this rule to allocate your expenditures no matter how much money you have.

Another way of dealing with expenditures to ensure that you do not overspend is using what we call "the envelope system". In this method, you simply allocate a certain amount of money to a particular expenditure then put the money in an envelope. Ensure that every type of expenditure has its envelope. For instance, you can have an envelope for groceries, utilities, entertainment, and such. Each time you remove a certain amount from a particular envelope, you know how much money is remaining, and you can realign your expenditures. This system is very effective in ensuring you don't overspend and in reducing how much you use your credit cards.

Personal Budget Worksheet

You can make use of the worksheet below to create your own personalized budget.

Recreate the table in Microsoft excel (or click on the link at the end of the table) to help you to do the calculations easily. Simply enter the estimated monthly income and expenses in the respective column to help you understand what it is you need to do to live within your budget. You can even add some more rows related to your income sources or expense items.

PART 1: MONTHLY INCOME	Estimated	Actual
Person #1: List monthly income for all full & part time jobs	$3,000.00	$3,000.00
Person #2: List monthly income for all full & part time jobs	$1,000.00	$1,000.00
Person #1: Unemployment Insurance (if applicable)	$0.00	$0.00
Person #2: Unemployment Insurance (if applicable)	$0.00	$0.00
Other: Child Support	$0.00	$0.00
Other: Tax Credits	$0.00	$0.00
Other: Incoming Rent for rental property	$1,000.00	$1,000.00
Other: List other income you'd like to track	$500.00	$500.00
TOTALS (Automatically Calculated)	*$5,500.00*	*$5,500.00*

Budgeting

PART 2: MONTHLY EXPENSE	Estimated	Actual
Mortgage / Rent	$1,000.00	$1,000.00
Home Equity Loan / Line Of Credit	$0.00	$0.00
Home Insurance	$25.00	$25.00
Credit Card #1	$100.00	$100.00
Credit Card #2	$75.00	$75.00
Credit Card #3	$45.00	$45.00
Credit Card #4 (add as many as you need to)	$25.00	$25.00
Car Payment	$200.00	$200.00
Car Insurance	$65.00	$65.00
Parking	$50.00	$50.00
Tolls	$80.00	$80.00
Gasoline	$60.00	$120.00
Subway		$0.00
Health Insurance	$45.00	$45.00
Cable / Satellite TV	$55.00	$55.00
Internet Access	$60.00	$60.00
Phone Bill	$0.00	$0.00
Mobile Phone Bill(s)	$35.00	$95.00
Daycare/Babysitting/Eldercare	$0.00	$45.00
Groceries	$100.00	$210.00
Pet care	$0.00	$20.00
Gym Membership	$0.00	$0.00

Jenny Holmquist

Heating	$25.00	$25.00
Electric Bill	$50.00	$80.00
Water Bill	$25.00	$30.00
Lawn Care	$0.00	$0.00
Unplanned: Vet Bill		$250.00
Unplanned: Dinner party		$70.00
Unplanned: Car repairs		$2,550.00
Unplanned: Parking Ticket		$75.00
Unplanned: Dishwasher repair		$450.00
Other		$0.00
TOTALS (Automatically Calculated)	$2,120.00	$5,845.00

PART 3: RESULTS (Automatically Generated from Parts 1 & 2 Above)	Estimated	Actual
TOTAL MONTHLY INCOME	$5,500.00	$5,500.00
TOTAL MONTHLY EXPENSE	$2,120.00	$5,845.00
VARIANCE (This is how much over, or under, your budget you are.)	$3,380.00	($345.00)

Source:

http://www.kiplinger.com/tool/spending/T007-S001-budgeting-worksheet-a-household-budget-for-today-a/

Chapter 3: Monitoring And Evaluation Of Your Budget

Managing finances does not end with having a good budget. You need to monitor and evaluate your budget constantly. Therefore, a good budget has to be flexible. Nothing is certain in life and changes may occur from time to time; hence, when you are constantly monitoring and evaluating, you can make adjustments and improvements whenever necessary.

Some common circumstances that might require you to make changes to your budget include:

- **Getting a Raise**: Getting a raise means that there is an increase in your income and the money within your disposal. You must therefore decide on how you want to be spending this increased income.

- **Loss of Job or Source of Income**: If you lose your job or a source of income, it would affect your budget; therefore, you must ensure that your budget reflects this change by adjusting the income part of your budget and then reducing your expenses to fit your income.

- **Financial Emergencies**: You might have provisions for financial emergencies in your budget but some financial emergencies can be bigger than you expect. For instance, if the wind blows off the roof of your house during a terrible storm and you don't have a house insurance cover, you might need to quickly fix the roof and this may cost a lot. In such situations, you would need to adjust your budget.

- **Big Purchases**: If you decide to purchase a house, a car or anything else that costs a lot of money, you also need to adjust your budget to be able to accommodate these expenses.

- **Major New Expense**: If you have a child going to college, that's a totally new expense that would be alien to your budget. This new cost must be reflected in your budget so you must adjust your budget to accommodate it.

- **Overhauling Your Social Life**: You may wake up one fine morning and decide your social life sucks and you want an overhaul. Cool idea but it would cost you money. You may need to start hanging out more, change your wardrobe, and get a new car and so on. All of these would also cost a lot, which might not be previously allowed for in your budget.

- **Lifestyle Changes**: Major lifestyle changes can also cost you a lot of money. For instance, if you decide you want to lose weight and start eating healthy, you have to spend more on gym subscriptions, whole foods, organic foods and other things that would help you achieve your goals fast.

- **Getting Rid of An Expense:** Assuming that your daughter or son graduates from college, you will no longer need to pay tuition fees and incur other college-related expenses. This major expense has to get off your list so you can free up money for other important expenses.

Evaluating And Improving Your Personal Budget

It doesn't just stop at creating a budget. Personal budget evaluation is something that you must continue to do to ensure that your budget continues to meet your goals. You see, financial goals can change over time. For instance, when you first created your budget, your goal might have been to reduce your debts or even to be completely free of debts. So let's say after six months of strictly sticking to your budget, you are able to pay off the debts and you are now debt free. That would render your current budget irrelevant and you must therefore begin to consider improving on your budget so that it can reflect the new goals you now have.

Some of the steps to take in order to evaluate and improve your budget include the following:

1. **Understand Your Current Goals**: Take a good look at what your new goals are. For instance, you are now free of debts so what next? Do you want to start planning for your retirement now? It is always important to review your goals every few months and ensure that it reflects in your budget.

2. **Is Your Current Budget Helping you Meet Those Goals**: If your financial goals have changed, you must ensure that the budget you are working on gives room for you to achieve your new goals. For instance, you may have to review your expenses to include certain expenses that are geared towards meeting your new financial goals or you may have to cut back on your current expenses so that you are able to save more.

3. **Improve Your Savings Strategy**: Many people always find it difficult to stick to a savings plan. They save some money

and then at the slightest chance, they tap into their savings and end up ruining their plans. If this is what has been happening with you, you should consider changing your savings strategy by maybe putting your money somewhere where it would be much more difficult to access.

4. **Assess Your Budget To see If It Is Still Working For You**: Is this budget easy to follow? If it's not, why? How can you improve on it or tweak it to make it much more realistic and relevant?

5. **Incorporate Free Money for Splurges**: If you don't include some free money in your budget that you can spend as you wish, it may make it difficult for you to stick with it. You must make some allowances for some money that you can spend as you see fit.

Monitoring And Sticking To Your Budget

Another very important aspect of budgeting is budget monitoring. You need to continue to monitor your budget so that you can be sure that you are getting the best value for your money.

Some steps you should take in order to monitor your budget include:

1. **Classify Your Expenses into Needs and Wants**: Food, shelter, clothing are examples of expenses that can fit into the category of needs because they are very essential to your existence. However, things like eating out, going on dates, cable TV, and expenses made on your hobbies are just wants meaning that you can do without them without your life being affected. Therefore, you must classify every single item in your budget into needs and wants.

2. **Are You Getting the Best Value for Your Money**: The next thing to do is to do a cost-benefit analysis for all the items you spend money on especially your needs. Are you getting the best value for your money? Are you overpaying for some items and if you are; how can you reduce such expenditure?

3. **Are Your Wants Relevant to Your Lifestyle and Goals**: The next thing you should consider is the relevance of your wants to your overall lifestyle and goals? If you are spending on cosmetics for instance, how does it help your lifestyle and help you achieve your goals in the long run?

4. **Understand The Timeframe For Every Expense**: Are the expenses permanent or temporary? If they are temporary, how can you adjust your budget so that you are able to get the best out of such expenses?

5. **Are there any duplicated expenses**: Are you spending money on something that might have already been paid for? For instance, if your spouse works and has health insurance benefits, you may not need to also pay for health insurance again.

After considering all the factors mentioned above, you should think of how to adjust your budget. You can consider eliminating or reducing some expenses which you think are not relevant or that do not fit into your long term plans. You can also consider changing service providers if you find out that you can get better offers somewhere else.

If you notice that a particular expense item keeps increasing, talk to your service provider. Ask them for the reasons for the increase and talk to them about what you can do to keep those costs from going up. You would be surprised that most service providers would be willing to offer you useful tips and advice.

Remember that in budgeting, every dollar counts so you must always keep an eye on your budget and ensure that you always get the best value for your money.

Let us now look at some tips that will help you stick to your budget.

Tips To Help You Stick To Your Budget

Preparing a budget is not difficult but sticking to a budget is. Following a budget requires financial discipline and determination on your part.

Some of these tips and tricks can help you improve your ability to stick to your budget plans without distractions and deviations.

1. **Don't spend what you don't have**: If you can't afford it, forget about it or wait until you have cash to pay for it. Don't pull your credit card out at the slightest opportunity you have to buy something that you can't afford.

2. **Always use a grocery list**: A grocery list helps you to avoid impulse buying and overspending. Make sure you create a master grocery list that you can always use whenever you want to go shopping.

3. **Keep and review all receipts**: Don't throw your receipts away. Keep them so that you can use them to review your spending pattern and understand the areas where you need to improve and adjust.

4. **Talk yourself out of impulse purchases**: Impulse buying is one of the greatest things that can defeat a budget plan. You must therefore talk yourself out of such impulse buying whenever you are tempted.

5. **Avoid commercials**: The media has made it increasingly difficult to stick to a budget, not with all those commercials tempting you to buy one new thing or the other. If you realize that commercials get you easily, avoid them completely.

6. **Always remind yourself of the benefits of sticking to your budget:** Whenever you are tempted to deviate from your budget, you should always remind yourself of the benefits of sticking to your budget such as achievement of your long-term financial goals.

7. **Use credit cards carefully**: Use your credit cards only when there is an emergency. Actually, when trying to manage your finances, you should get rid of your credit cards and only have 1 or two credit cards for emergencies only.

8. **Sleep on your purchases**: Before you spend money on anything big, spend some time thinking about it carefully.

9. **Avoid wastage**: Don't waste anything. Make sure that any item you purchase is completely used up before you purchase another one.

10. **Understand that your expenses are a reflection of your personality**: The way you spend money says a lot about who you are and how your life is going to turn out in the future. You might want to consider this detail whenever you are tempted to deviate from your budget.

11. **Respect money**: Understand that money is a sacred thing that has to be judiciously used, managed and passed on to

generations and not just something to throw around and waste.

12. **Research before purchasing**: Before you purchase any item, do a proper research. Compare prices, research quality, and durability to save costs.

13. **Motivate and reward yourself**: Look for ways to reward yourself when you discover that you have successfully stuck to your budget after a period of time.

Chapter 4: Expenses That Affect Your Budget and How to Tackle Them

There are a number of expenses that you should keep your eye on as they could destroy your budget and make you get less value for your money.

1. **Cable bills**: Most people spend an average of $80 every month on cable bills. You might be able to avoid such expenses by using internet-based media like Netflix, YouTube and Hulu to satisfy your entertainment needs.

2. **Cell phone contracts**: Expensive long-term contracts can mess with your budget. Instead of expensive 2-year contracts, go for low-cost phone contracts with no long-term commitments.

3. **Heating bills**: Heating equipment sap a lot of energy and you may soon find out that your heating bills always overshoot budgeted costs. However, you can reduce your heating bills just by turning down the thermostat.

4.**Transportation costs**: Expenses on gas and vehicle maintenance can also accumulate over time so you should consider taking public transportation sometimes to reduce such expenses.

5.**Lunch and eat-outs**: Packing a lunch bag with you to work can help you save a lot of money that would rather have been spent on lunch and other eat-outs.

6.**Gym Subscriptions**: Costs of gym subscriptions when added up over time can be used to purchase gym equipment that could be used at home. You should consider investing in your own gym equipment so that you are able to exercise at home.

7. **Grocery shopping**: Doing your grocery shopping in a retail store can be very expensive compared to buying wholesale. You may be able to save a lot of money in a year just from buying groceries in bulk.

8. **Morning coffee**: You would be surprised at how much that cup of latte accumulates to at the end of the month. Consider making your own coffee at home instead of buying.

9.**Medications:** Prescription drugs can also make your wallet go lean very fast. Consider substituting your prescription drugs for generic drugs to save money. Generics are the bio-equivalent of brand-name drugs, but cost 80 to 85 percent less. You can also sign up for a pharmacy loyalty card so that you can take advantage of discounts offered.

10. **Entertainment and hang outs:** Date nights can cost you a lot of money. Look for cheaper entertainment options.

11.   **Clothing:** Do you really need that designer shirt when you can get a good quality shirt for a fraction of those brand names?

Common Budget Mistakes To Avoid

1. **Setting a budget that is too rigid:** Your budget should not seem like a prison sentence. It should very flexible and open to change.

2. **Forgetting your savings**: Do not ever make the mistake of leaving savings out of your budgeting equation. Savings turn out to be lifesavers in the long run.

3. **Not Reviewing Your Budget:** I already mentioned the benefits of monitoring and evaluating your budget. You should always ensure that you review each item on your budget and make necessary adjustments regularly.

4. **Too Frugal:** Don't create a budget that lets you live a miserly life or a lifestyle that is too far from what you are used to otherwise, it wouldn't be long before that budget ends up in a trash can.

In the following chapter, we will look at online budgeting tools that can be of great help in coming up with a great budget and help you manage your finances.

Chapter 5: Online Budgeting Tools

You can make the process of creating your personal budget a lot faster and easier by making use of any of these online budgeting and personal finance tools:

They are all free and easy to use.

1. **Mint.com**: It is an online-based budgeting tool that allows you to link your financial accounts to it such as your savings, checking and credit card accounts. It automatically updates your information as they appear in your account and can be used to track spending, debt management and provide insight into your finances.

2. **Personal Capital**: Personal capital helps you to track your investments and other parts of your budget. It has a financial budget that helps you to clearly see what is happening in your financial life and track your investments portfolio.

3. **Chase Blueprint**: If you use credit cards a lot, this one's for you. It offers budgeting plans that pair with your credit card.

It also offers you a personalized plan that helps to pay off your debts, reduce interest payments, and monitor your spending pattern.

4. **Budget Pulse**: This one also helps you to visualize your budget and spending patterns using graphs and charts as well as helps you to monitor your spending against your goals.

5. **Buxfer**: Buxfer can be used to keep track of upcoming bills along with goal setting and financial planning.

Other popular online budgeting tools that you can use include Money Strands, Money Tracker, My Spending Plan, Budget Simple and Savvy Money.

Conclusion

The key to successful budgeting is flexibility and discipline. When your budget is flexible enough and reflects a lifestyle you are used to, it would be easier to follow, but when it is too rigid and kind of makes you live miserably, its dead on arrival.

Always create a budget that you would enjoy and make sure you are disciplined enough to stick with it.

Thank you again for taking the time to read this book!

I hope this book was able to help you to learn about budgeting and how to create an effective budget.

The next step is to put what you have leant into action.

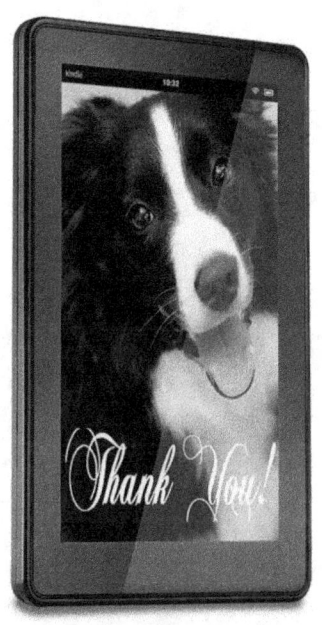

Finally, if you enjoyed this book, would you be kind enough to leave a review for this book?

Thank you and good luck!

www.ingramcontent.com/pod-product-compliance
Lightning Source LLC
Chambersburg PA
CBHW071834200526
45169CB00018B/1474